First Communion

A Parish Celebration

Developed by
James Bitney

Family Book

St. Anthony Messenger Press
AND FRANCISCAN COMMUNICATIONS
Cincinnati, Ohio

Nihil Obstat: David A. Dillon, S.T.D.

Imprimatur: +John R. Roach, D.D.
Archbishop of St. Paul
and Minneapolis
November 21, 1980

ISBN 0-86716-267-8 (formerly ISBN 86683-101-1,
0-03-058664-X and 1-55944-038-4)

Printed in the United States of America

Project Editor: Yvette Nelson

Designer: Sally Brewer

Editorial Assistance: Sandra Sella

Consultants:
Michael Joncas, associate pastor and liturgist
Dolores Curran, author and columnist on the family
and the Church

Illustrations:
James Arnosky, pages 14, 15, 26, 27, 34, 35, 36.
Chris Larson, pages 21, 22, 23.
Maria Mazzara, pages 39, 40, 41, 42, 43, 44.
Suzanne Schaffhausen, pages 9, 10, 11, 12.
Kathryn Shoemaker, cover, pages 7, 19, 24, 29, 33, 3*

Photographs:
Jim LaVigne, page 31, upper left, lower right.
John Maines, page 31, lower left.
Michael Paul, pages 17; 18; 32, lower right.
Cyril A. Reilly, page 13, upper left, center, lower righ*
              lower left; page 31, upper right; page
              32, upper left, upper right, lower left.
Cheryl Walsh-Belville, page 13, upper right.

ST. ANTHONY MESSENGER PRESS
AND FRANCISCAN COMMUNICATIONS
1615 Republic Street
Cincinnati, OH 45210-1298
(513) 241-5615

Contents

The Family and the Parish Together

Your family is the primary and fundamental source of your child's faith development. We rest secure when we know that our children are being raised in healthy and loving families; instinctively we know that our Church, as well as our society, depends on healthy families. Where family life is threatened, we rally to stave off the eroding influences. Where family ties are missing, we attempt to introduce social groupings and caring bonds based on family models.

Similarly, the celebration of the Eucharist forms the heart and source of the parish's faith life. A healthy local church centers itself in eucharistic celebration. All other parish activities flow from and return to the community's sense of itself as a people who celebrate "the death of the Lord until he comes." We recognize this inherent gift and power of the Eucharist, and consequently, we feel slighted when the Eucharist is celebrated in a casual, perfunctory, or hurried manner.

First Communion, A Parish Celebration gathers these two life sources—your family in its daily life and the parish family in its eucharistic celebration—to welcome your child to Communion. This program places the final preparation and celebration of First Communion squarely in the home and in the parish church—around the hearth and table, and around the Word and the Bread.

For its inspiration and impetus, *First Communion, A Parish Celebration* looks back to the rich tradition of the early Church and ahead to the implementation of the newly revised *Rite of Christian Initiation of Adults*. From the richness of the past and with a mandate which looks to the future, this program invites your family and the parish community to come together in communion in a way that is ever new and ever renewing.

The early Church invited people who were interested in Christianity to join them on a journey of faith. Those who responded to this invitation became candidates for initiation, or catechumens. As they shared the faith-filled life of the Christian community, the candidates discovered and began living out Gospel values. The step-by-step initiation process was called the *catechumenate*.

During this time of coming to faith, the early Church prayed for and with the catechumens and celebrated the stages of their faith journey with rituals of welcome and belonging. The early Church joyfully recognized the culmination of the catechumens' instruction and welcomed them into the saving reality of the paschal mystery by celebrating the Sacraments of Intitiation—Baptism, Confirmation, Eucharist—at the solemn Vigil of Easter, the great Paschal Feast. The Christian community born of the death and resurrection of Christ and continually sustained and renewed in the ritual celebration of that paschal mystery, celebrated throughout Eastertide, until Pentecost day.

Today the Church is rediscovering this ancient way of initiating new members. It is becoming more and more aware of the meaning and the importance of the Sacraments of Initiation. The Second Vatican Council called for the restoration of the order of the Sacraments of Initiation. Acting on the Council's direction, the Congregation for Divine Worship issued the new *Rite of Christian Initiation of Adults* in 1972. The *Rite*, which is just beginning to find its way into the life of the local parish community, promises to revitalize the whole Church. For the Church sees initiation and the lifelong conversion it implies as the beginning of a journey, not as an isolated moment. The *Rite* shifts the focus from the individual to the community. It calls for a vibrant community of faith in which the newly initiated can grow toward Christian wholeness. The candidates begin and continue their faith journey in a vital and supportive environment, rather than in an exclusively informational setting.

When you help your child prepare for First Communion, you are, in fact, initiating him or her into the life of the eucharistic community. In a sense, this initiation has "catechumenal" overtones.

Since children preparing for First Communion have been baptized in infancy, they are already members of the Christian family. They have grown up in the faith and now are coming to a fuller participation in the life of the Church.

Children gradually come to an awareness of

the ritual of the Eucharist through education and through celebration. By worshiping together as a family, your child has become rooted in the rituals and the faith stories of the Church. These experiences of the eucharistic celebration (formation) bring to life the content your child has learned about the Eucharist.* The effectiveness of formal religious education and eucharistic celebration multiplies when it builds on your family's lived faith. At the same time the community's prayerful support, its comprehension of the Good News, and its style of living out that Good News all feed the faith of the first communicant.

In sum, this program helps prepare children for First Communion not by simply informing them about the Eucharist, but rather by initiating them into the Body of Christ through the parish's Sunday celebration of the Eucharist and through the at-home sessions in this *Family Book*.

At the same time, through four *Communal Ritual Celebrations*, the worshiping community witnesses to its faith and to the faith journey of your child and the other children preparing for First Communion. On each of four consecutive Sundays the parish community prays with and for your family and welcomes you into a deeper relationship with God by inviting your child to participate in the Sacrament of Eucharist. As you can see, this approach to the Sacrament of Eucharist is by no means new. Rather, it is the most basic approach we know, and the one to which the new *Rite* happily invites us to return.

As parents, then, your first task and privilege is to be parents—to be models of lived faith active in love, rather than teachers of the content of faith. Children model their lives on the lives of adults who are important to them. They also model the faith of older adults as they grow toward choosing their own relationship and commitment to God. This is why it matters more that your family prays together than which prayers you say—why it matters more that your family worships together at Mass than what you know about the renewal of the liturgy. It matters that your child grows up visiting the old, taking food to the bereaved, seeing dignity in all people. It matters that your children grow up loved—consistently treated, talked to, trusted, played with, challenged to care, and valued in your family.

The bonds between you and your children are marked by the special poignancy of their openness with you and your hopes for them. When you share your own faith and invite your children to grow up in that faith, you also experience God's invitation to a deeper relationship. Children's openness and sometimes wide-eyed expectations of you call you to clarify your faith, to simplify it to its bare bones; from this can come a profound deepening of your relationship with God and a growing consciousness of whom and what you really value.

*The writers of this program assume that second graders participate in formal education either in the parish day school or in the religious education center, which likely uses one of the major curricula that centers on the Eucharist and the Mass in grade two.

This *Family Book* contains four at-home sessions: *We Celebrate Sunday, We Remember Jesus, We Share a Special Meal, We Celebrate as God's Thankful Family.* To better understand the program, read over the entire book before beginning with your child. Each of the four sessions includes a parent page which includes the session's *Aim* and the *Overview.* The *Aim* clarifies the purpose of each session, and the *Overview* provides background reflections and sets the direction for each session. *Parent Notes* are printed on the lower border of the children's pages and are indicated by the symbol ●●. These special helps, ideas, methods, and examples will guide you as you share the activities and discussions with your child. In consulting the *Parent Notes,* follow your intuition and choose what

is comfortable for your family; you know your child best. The main section of each of the four sessions directly addresses your child. The photographs, illustrations, stories, and activities are planned to meet the abilities and capabilities of your second-grader.

As soon as feasible, have a small family meeting. Commit yourself to set aside a time each week to involve your family in these at-home sessions. The days run by too quickly, and unless these at-home sessions are scheduled and faithfully kept, Saturday night will arrive and catch you unprepared for the Sunday *Communal Ritual Celebration.* In any case, these at-home meetings will further your child's growth as a faithful person. He or she will long remember that you gathered together to prepare for First Communion—to pray together and to talk about God and Jesus. Your child will remember these times together more vividly than formal classroom instructions. These memories of preparation and care at home will stay in the mind, the heart, and the emotions of your growing child.

The *Communal Ritual Celebrations* form the other half of this First Communion preparation. The Sunday celebrations complement the at-home sessions. Each celebration follows your family's at-home session. In broad focus within the parish family, the ritual celebrates the faith that has been shared in the intimate circle of your home during the preceding week. Within the Sunday eucharistic liturgy, the theme of each at-home session is highlighted. In this way, the faith community is invited to offer its prayers and support by ritually marking your child's steps to the eucharistic table. Through this series of four public expressions of welcome, which culminate in First Communion, you, as a first communicant family, receive the support of the parish family and also give public witness to the journey of faith you are making with your child.

We Celebrate Sunday, the first *Communal Ritual Celebration,* focuses on Sabbath time. In this session we thank God for the generous gift of sacred time, and enroll the children as candidates for First Communion.

In the second celebration, *We Remember Jesus,* the children receive a candle as a reminder of their Baptism and as a sign to help them remember the gift of Jesus.

Bread is given to the children at the third celebration, *We Share a Special Meal.* They are asked to share the bread at a meal with their families and to remember that they are called to the special meal Jesus gives to God's family.

The fourth celebration, *We Celebrate as God's Thankful Family,* invites the candidates to partake of the Body and Blood of the Lord. On behalf of the entire community, the children are presented with a formal invitation to receive Holy Communion.

In summary, we've seen that you as parents have always watched over your child's faith since Baptism. You've taken care that your child has been enrolled in the formal religious education programs available in your parish community. You've relied on these programs to build on and support the faith which is daily lived in your home. You've gathered as families to celebrate the Eucharist.

Now, the faith community (your parish) gathers to help you prepare and to celebrate the initiation of your child to First Communion. The parish community has a stake in these young children and a commitment to their future. It's fitting that the community which has supported these last steps to full participation in the Eucharist will participate in the full celebration on the day of First Communion—truly a parish event, a day in which the parish family can be glad and rejoice.

1.
We Celebrate Sunday

Blessed are you, O Lord.
You make us Easter people.
You give us special times to celebrate.
You send Jesus to help us remember your love.
You invite us to share the special meal of Jesus.
We thank you, Lord, for all your gifts,
and we bless your name forever.
Amen.

Aim

Your child will explore the ways in which Sunday is a special day for your family. Your child will recognize that Sunday is a special day because on that day we celebrate the resurrection of Jesus.

Overview

Have you ever noticed the differences between the days of the week? Mondays, for example, seem to be hard-starting, engine-sticking days; days when we need to push ourselves a little harder than usual to get going. However, once Wednesday is passed, the remainder of the week seems all down hill, and on Fridays we begin to unwind. The work week does not blaze out; rather, it trickles away as we clear our desks or finish the housework, all in preparation for the weekend. While Saturday is not a day of work for most of us, we usually fill the day with our own routine business—we shop or putter around the house, maybe we get ready for an evening out.

Sunday, however, seems to be a really different day in our week. Even the newspaper is larger and the comics are in color. Our day takes on a more leisurely pace. Perhaps we sleep later or make a special breakfast after Mass. Outside our homes, the traffic has thinned, there are no rush hours on this day, and many stores are closed. If we live on the farm, we notice that life slows down. We still have to do the milking, but we weigh more seriously the necessity of plowing the fields on Sunday.

Why this change of pace? Sabbath reaches back to the liberation of the Hebrews from exile and the covenant on Mount Sinai. The Hebrews were no longer an anxious and enslaved people. They no longer had to bear the grim, futureless burden of slavery. They were God's own free people. They celebrated this freedom with a day of rest and worship each week.

For the Christian community the resurrection of Jesus marks Sunday as an extraordinary day. On Sunday we celebrate that Easter experience which has changed our lives irrevocably. We belong to the redeemed community of the Risen Lord. We are free and we are loved. We know once and for all that this is a special day the Lord has made, and we're able to rejoice and be glad in it.

Children are aware of the changes that happen on Sunday. From their own family and parish experiences, children recognize that Sunday is different. In this first session you'll explore the various ways in which Sunday is different for your family.

The fable *Sabbath*, on page 9, reminds us all of the graceful gift of time to remember who we are and whose we are. You'll be invited to talk with your child about the time he or she values. Time often will be important simply because you share it with your child.

After reading the story *The Resurrection*, on page 14, with your child, you'll be invited to consider other ways to celebrate Sunday as a family. You may be surprised to discover what your child most enjoys, most regards as special.

The closing page of this week's session offers suggestions for welcoming and closing Sunday in your home.

This focus on Sunday makes it possible for all of us to mark the celebration of the resurrection which sheds its light on our whole week. As we're reminded in the movie, *A Thousand Clowns*, "You got to know what day it is . . . You have to own your days and name them, . . . or else the years go right by and none of them belongs to you." Sunday is the day when we stand together before God, a day when we are free enough to play a little.

Sabbath

A Fable — by James Bitney

The face of the great clock looked down on the village square and struck the hour. "Bong! Bong! Bong!" it chimed and echoed off the distant, misty mountain. "Bong! Bong! Bong!" sounded the echo. Only one hour to wait!

Each year on this special afternoon all the villagers gathered to stare wide-eyed at the great clock. Each year they waited for four o'clock, "the hour of the gift"—the time of the king's birthday. THE CLOCK STRUCK THE QUARTER HOUR!

Shoemakers left their shops, bakers left their ovens, children left their schools. Housewives left their washing on the line. Telephone operators left people on the line. Everyone stopped what they were doing to be in the square by four o'clock, because it was the king's birthday.

Now you might think that all these people would be bringing presents, wouldn't you? But that was not the case at all! No, even as four o'clock came nearer— not a single present was present.

What? No gifts for the king? Whose birthday was it anyway? Why was the square so crowded with empty-handed people?

But this was not unusual. It was the same last year and the year before and the year before that. You see, year after year on the king's birthday everyone gathered under the clock in the shadow of the misty mountain, and, at four o'clock, the king gave the people a gift!

•• **Parent Notes**

*To consider the importance of the gift of time, read the fable, **Sabbath,** with your child. Before the reading, recall that you shared this story at the Family Meeting which began the First Communion program.*

THE CLOCK STRUCK THE HALF HOUR!

All of the people shifted their weight from one foot to the other. All eyes grew even wider, staring at the clock. Each person wondered what the king would give this year.

THE CLOCK STRUCK THE THREE-QUARTER HOUR!

No one spoke, and that was normal for this crowd. No one waved a hand or smiled a smile. No one had done any of these things yesterday either, or the day before, or even last week. In fact, the people never gathered together at all except on this one day each year, and even then, no one spoke.

The people weren't angry with one another. They just really didn't know one another, and they didn't see any reason why they should. As a matter of fact, the people didn't even know the king himself! Each year the king gave them a gift, but the people never saw him, never talked to him, never thanked him! This was normal in the village, but it was very odd!

THE HANDS OF THE CLOCK POINTED TO FOUR AND TWELVE!

Each person's heart skipped a beat. The clock was about to strike the hour; the gift about to be given.

But then something not very normal at all happened. Actually, something very normal didn't happen. The clock did not chime! Its hands just relaxed and stopped! The people turned to the clock in the bakery and the clock in the shoemaker's shop. They had also stopped! What

had happened? What did it mean?

The people turned to one another. "What shall we do?" they asked. "Should we wait? Will the king still give his gift? What shall we do?"

For the first time since the mist covered the mountain, since the great clock began to tick, the people didn't know what to do, and that was odd! But also, for the first time in memory, the people noticed one another. The shoemaker noticed the baker, the housewife noticed her children.

"What shall we do?" they all asked each other. "I know," piped a small voice.

Quickly the people turned to see a little boy with large brown eyes. "I know," he repeated. "Let's do nothing, or just anything at all!"
NOTHING!!
ANYTHING
AT ALL!!

In normal times the people would never listen to a child. But this was no normal time. The great clock had stopped. All the clocks had stopped! And the people had done something they had never done before. They had actually noticed one another. So the bright-eyed little boy's idea didn't seem odd at all, even to people who were always busy doing something.

The baker opened his shop and gave away cookies and pies. Picnics sprung up everywhere. People told stories, walked walks, held hands, and shared the baker's goodies. And no one worried about what the king would give them any more!

In fact, people started to talk about gifts for the king. Gaily wrapped presents began to appear at the foot of the clock. The people began to cheer and dance, as if all birthdays were happening at once. They sang "Happy Birthday" to the king, and their song flew through the valley.

While the people celebrated, time—as it always does—flew by, twenty-four hours of it! As they sang the birthday song, the hands of the great clock suddenly began to move again. The clock struck the hour, "Bong! Bong! Bong! Bong!"

O what a day! A day to be remembered and repeated! The people shouted, "We must do this again!"

"Let's do it again next week!" cheered the children.

And that is just what they did. Every week, week after week, the people gathered under the clock to celebrate and praise the king.

And something else happened, something very odd indeed. The mist on the mountain disappeared! And from its top the king looked down on his people—his so-deep brown eyes twinkling. No longer would his people gather only once a year on his birthday to receive. Now they would gather every week to give—to the king and to one another.

The king had given his final gift, but it was the greatest gift of all!

THE END

BUT REALLY, ONLY THE BEGINNING!

●● *Help your child review the answers to the questions which were asked at the Family Meeting:* **What were the people like before the king gave his gift? What were the people like after the gift was given?**

Families celebrate together.

●● *Direct your child's attention to the above pictures of families sharing leisure time together. Use the pictures as a springboard to help your child think of Sunday activities which are special to your family.*

The Resurrection

Very early on Sunday morning, Mary Magdalene and two other women went to Jesus' tomb. They were friends of Jesus. They found the tomb empty. The stone that closed the tomb was rolled away. Mary ran to Jesus' friends, Peter and John. "Someone has taken Jesus!" Mary told them. Peter, John, and Mary ran back to the tomb. It was empty. They were confused and didn't know what to do. Peter and John went home, but Mary stayed near the tomb. A man came by.

"Where have you put Jesus?" Mary asked.

"Mary," the man said.

Mary knew the man was Jesus when he said her name. Mary ran to tell Jesus' other friends.

"I have seen Jesus!" she said.

That evening Jesus appeared to Peter and John and many of his other friends. Jesus was alive. His Father had raised Jesus up to new life.

Mary, Peter, John, and the other apostles are witnesses to Jesus' new life!

adapted from John 20:1-18

●● *Ask your child to tell you in his or her own words the story of Jesus' resurrection. (Most children will have learned something of the story from religion class or from their experience of Easter.)*

After your child has told the story in his or her way, talk a little about the day of the week on which the Resurrection happened. Then read the above story, **The Resurrection,** *with your child.*

●● *After reading the story make a simple statement which tells why we as Catholic Christians keep Sunday special. Examples are, "On Sunday we celebrate the day of Jesus' resurrection," or "Our celebration of Jesus' resurrection makes Sunday a special day for us."*

We celebrate Sunday as a family.

- We shine shoes on Saturday night.
- We settle squabbles before going to bed.
- We prepare for Mass by reading the Gospel for the day.
- We eat a different kind of breakfast like pancakes rather than cold cereal.
- We go out for breakfast.
- We read the funny papers together.
- We visit family friends and relatives.
- We postpone all quarreling.
- We have a special food.
- We use our best dishes.
- We have a special treat like popcorn or ice cream at night.

_____

_____

_____

To make our Sunday special, our family has decided to

_____

•• _Use the above suggestions to help you think about your family's Sunday celebration. Ask your family members how they want to make Sunday special._

Add new suggestions to the list. Then, review the whole list together, and as a family decide to do one or two of these activities to mark Sunday as special.

We welcome Sunday.

Parent: **B**lessed are you Father, for giving us this special day to celebrate together as a family. This is the day you raised Jesus from the dead!

All: **F**ather, may this day be a time of togetherness and joy for our family.

Amen.

●●*Begin a family tradition by welcoming Sunday with prayer. Place a candle on the kitchen or dining room table and gather your family. After you have led the first part of the above prayer, light the candle and invite everyone to complete the prayer. Then extinguish the candle.*

We thank God for Sunday.

We praise God for Sunday!
God gives us this day
to share with others
in prayer and in play.
It is now Sunday evening,
and as shadows grow deep,
we bless God for all great gifts
as we go to sleep.

Amen.

●● *To bring Sunday to a peaceful close, gather your family around the table before bedtime, light the candle again, and join hands as you say the above evening prayer of thanksgiving for Sunday.*

Looking Ahead to Sunday

Tell your child that on the following Sunday he or she will be welcomed by the people at church. During the Mass all of the children who will be receiving *First Communion will be asked to sign their names in a special book. Soon they will be ready to receive Holy Communion.*

2.

We Remember Jesus

Blessed are you, O Lord.
You make us Easter people.
You give us special times to celebrate.
You send Jesus to help us remember your love.
You invite us to share the special meal of Jesus.
We thank you, Lord, for all your gifts,
and we bless your name forever.
Amen.

Aim

Your child will recognize that by remembering we keep people and events alive and effectively present. Your child will remember stories about Jesus which are present in the Christian family.

Overview

Have you ever felt lost or out of place? Maybe you confused directions on a journey. Perhaps you were in a quandary over a personal relationship. Confronted with such situations, most of us stop and take a closer look at where we are, where we've been, and what we were trying to do. In a word, we remember.

You will recall that in the story, *Sabbath,* the people were quite a sorry lot before the king gave his gift. Although they regarded themselves as normal, they were lost and out of place. They had forgotten their heritage—that memory of the basic relationships which told them who they were and how they related to one another. Consequently, no real vision of the future remained for them. It took a special gift of time to force them to reestablish their fundamental relationships, and so to help them remember who and whose they were, where they were heading, and what their life together should be about.

In our society today, we've come to a deeper awareness of the importance of remembering. The television dramas, *Roots* and *Holocaust* taught us that. We've learned that remembering can be both a blessing and a curse; it can make us happy or sad. Memory can lull us into complacency so that we live in the past. Or memory can spur us to action, so that we live in the present, building on the richness of the past. Memory puts our present life in proper perspective. It helps us better understand the meaning of present events of our lives as well as the meaning of life itself.

When we look closely at the life of Jesus, we discover that much of his mission was to help us remember who God is, and in light of the revelation that God is Father, we know that we are called to be children of the Father and brothers and sisters to one another. In his life and in his words Jesus leads us to see that because God remembers us, our life in God is secure. In his death and resurrection we know that fullness of life forever is our heritage. As Christians we, then, are a people who have inherited powerful memories, and we are able to look forward to and follow a compelling vision of fullness of life in and with God.

Children love to know about the past. Perhaps your child has asked you to remember the "good old days" and tell about way back in the sixties! Children also enjoy retelling the stories they've heard and recalling the experiences they've had. In this session you'll have an opportunity to share with your child your recollections and to invite your child's recollections of events in his or her short life. By helping your child remember a special person or family experience and by sharing your recollections, you will help him or her to realize that story functions as a stabilizer and a firm ground in family life.

Similarly, you'll want to remember with your child some of the events in the life of Jesus. Primary school children have a small collection of stories about Jesus to draw from. By remembering together, you will help your child become more familiar with Jesus and more ready to understand how the story of God and his people is disclosed in the Old and New Testaments, why the Word is celebrated in every Eucharist, and why Jesus asked all of us to celebrate his death and resurrection at a Christian family meal with the invitation, "Do this in memory of me."

The Tennis Ball with the Funny Face

"Where is your brother Damon?" asked Mother. Rachel put her schoolbooks on the window ledge. "Oh, he's over at the school yard bouncing that old tennis ball of his," Rachel replied. "But he said he'd be home in time for supper." Mother wondered why Damon spent so much time playing alone with that tennis ball, but she kept her thoughts to herself.

Later that evening, Damon was helping Mother do the dishes. When he climbed on the kitchen stool and reached up to put away the soup bowls, something popped out of his pocket, fell to the floor, then bounced up on the counter and finally, splashed into the sink!

"Oh!" said Mother in surprise.

"My tennis ball!" cried Damon.

•• Parent Notes

This story will help your child recognize that remembering makes present someone who is far from us. Remembering also gives us hope for the future. To focus your child's attention on the purpose of the story, simply say that this is the story of a boy named Damon and how he remembered a special friend named Joshua.

Sure enough, there, floating like a big fuzzy soap bubble, was Damon's tennis ball. Quickly Mother fished it out of the sudsy water and started to wipe it off with a paper towel.

"The funny face!" shouted Damon. "Don't wipe off the funny face!" Mother looked at the tennis ball. It was dirty and smudged, but she could see a drawing of a funny face still on it. "It's all right, Damon," she said. "The face is still smiling." Mother spread a clean towel on the table and gently placed the tennis ball on it to dry.

When the kitchen was all cleaned, Mother turned to Damon and said, "You play with that ball every day, Damon. You must like it very much." "Uh hmm, I do," he whispered. "I wonder why?" asked Mother.

"Because of the funny face."

"The funny face?"

"Yes," Damon nodded, "cuz Joshua drew that face."

Suddenly Mother understood. Joshua had been Damon's best friend in first grade. But Joshua's father had to go to a new job in another town, so the whole family moved away. They would not come back for three whole years!

"Me and Joshua always used to play catch," said Damon. "So when he moved away, he gave me this tennis ball with the funny face he drew on it. Joshua was real good at playing catch and good at drawing too."

"When you play with the funny-face ball, do you sometimes think about Joshua?" Mother asked.

"Uh huh," Damon answered, "and when I bounce the ball, I remember Joshua and all the stuff we used to do. Sometimes I think the funny face kind of even looks like Joshua did when the teacher told him that he drew good pictures. It makes me feel good to remember that Joshua will come back when his daddy's job gets changed again."

"I have an idea," said Mother. "Why don't we write Joshua a letter? Let's write a letter to tell Joshua we remember him and look forward to seeing him again. And do you know what, Damon?"

"What, Mom?"

"I'll bet that you'll get a letter back from Joshua, because I'm sure that Joshua remembers you."

Mother smiled.

Damon smiled.

Do you know what he looked like?

He looked kind of like this!

●● After you've read the story with your child, invite him or her to tell what he or she thinks about Damon's way of remembering Joshua.

23

We remember special people.

A person that I especially remember is

_____.

This is a picture of the time when _____

_____.

●● *Talk with your child about people who are special to your family the way Joshua was special to Damon. These people can be friends, relatives, adults, children, and people who are far away or nearby.*

Ask your child to pick a person who is very special to him or her and fill in the first blank above.

Most often special people are tied to memorable events. Ask your child to fill in the second blank above and draw a picture of what she or he remembers about an event experienced with a special person.

Our family remembers.

We remember when

_____

_____

_____

_____.

We remember when

_____

_____

_____

_____.

●● Look over your family photos and decide with your child the ones he or she wishes to include on this page. (If you have a large collection of photos, you may want to select a limited number of photos ahead of time from which your child can choose.)

As your child selects photos, share your own remembrance of these events. Some events may have occurred when your child was too small to remember. Finally, help your child complete the sentences by each picture above.

We remember Jesus.

We remember when Jesus

_____

_____

_____ .

We remember when Jesus

_____

_____

_____ .

●● Help your child to see that because we belong to the family of Christians and because we're followers of Jesus, it's important that we know the Christian family stories of Jesus. Ask your child to tell you in his or her own words the stories that each picture suggests.

Then help your child complete the sentences by each picture on these two pages.

Blessed are you,
  Lord our God.
We are people who can
  remember our family stories.
Thank you for letting our
  family remember.
Thank you for letting us
  remember Jesus.
Jesus helps us remember
  how much you love us.
We love you too, Father,
  with Jesus and your Spirit.

Amen.

We remember when Jesus

_____

_____

_____.

●● *Use the above prayer to review the ideas presented in this session—we remember our family stories, and we remember our Christian family stories. In knowing our stories we know who we are, and we know whose we are.*

Ways we celebrate remembering.

- If you have a written family history, read or talk about it.

- Begin writing a family history if you don't have one.

- Record the voices of all the members of your family.

- Gather loose snapshots, cards, and other mementoes which you've been meaning to put in one place, and update your family scrapbook or photo album.

- Visit your family's "historical sites."

- Research and make a family tree.

- To keep alive the Christian family story, buy a Children's New Testament, and put it in a place of honor in your home.

●● *The above list gives various activities which will help keep your family memory alive and present.*

Looking Ahead to Sunday

Remind your child that at Mass this Sunday he or she will have another opportunity to remember Jesus. Tell your child that the community is planning to give each child who is preparing for First Communion a special gift to remind them of the love Jesus has for them.

3.

We Share a Special Meal

Blessed are you, O Lord.
You make us Easter people.
You give us special times to celebrate.
You send Jesus to help us remember your love.
You invite us to share the special meal of Jesus.
We thank you, Lord, for all your gifts,
and we bless your name forever.
Amen.

Aim

Your child will remember his or her own experiences of family meals and of festive meals. Your child will grow to appreciate that Jesus chose a meal in which to give himself to us.

Overview

By instinct we seem to realize that feeding is an act of love, whether it be the infant at the breast or the family gathered around the supper table. As human beings, eating means more to us than the satisfaction of physiological need. It implies intimacy and trust. That's why most of us don't relish eating alone or with strangers. At mealtime we prefer to be with those who share life, love, and purpose with us. We know that at mealtime, we share far more than food.

We live in an era of fast foods and instant dinners. We find our families more and more involved in activities outside the home, and the family mealtime has suffered as a consequence. Even though we look to family meals as important events, too often we find that they are hurried, harried, and hassled experiences. Rare is the parent who has not let escape the almost primal scream, "Can't we get through just one meal around here without spilling the milk?" Many of us have also experienced the wounding hostility that can slip out at mealtime, especially at festive meals. (It's important and comforting to remember that even Jesus experienced bickering and contention at his table, and even at the Last Supper!) Nonetheless, most of us still approach mealtime with expectancy, for it promises to be that one time each day when we can relax, enjoy, and celebrate the life, love, and purpose we share with one another.

Children know from their own experience that mealtimes are occasions for gathering and sharing. They are able to recognize that a meal is the work of many hands, and that thanks is appropriate. Children know that when families gather at the table, they have the opportunity to share the events of their day, to remember both the joys and the sorrows, the achievements and the failures. Once these are shared with others, joys are multiplied and burdens lifted or made easier to bear. Upon leaving the table, the family members know that they've been strengthened in body and spirit, and that now they're impelled to live a fuller life together. Many of the high points of Jesus' ministry occurred at meals. It was no accident that Jesus chose a meal—a gathering of friends who shared a common life and love—at which to reveal the depths of God's love for us. All the many dimensions of family and festive meals were included in the celebration of the Last Supper. Jesus focused these dimensions on a specific gift of God—he took simple bread and wine and indentified himself with them.

We view this action of Jesus from the perspective of our Easter experience of the resurrection, seeing him as the "Christ." We believe that by his word and gesture, the purpose and reality of bread and wine are changed and given new meaning and identity; Christ is with us here and now. We believe that sharing this meal means that the communion between God and us continues, that whenever we gather to break bread and share wine, Jesus is present.

In last week's session your child learned that memory makes special people and events present to us. In this session, by reviewing his or her own experiences of family and festive meals and by listening to the story of the Last Supper, your child will learn how Jesus asks us to remember him, how Jesus remembers us, and that Jesus gives himself for us, and is now present to us in Bread and Wine.

This coming Sunday your child will receive a gift of bread to share with your family after Sunday Mass (see *Looking Ahead to Sunday*, page 36). To make this sharing special, plan a family meal ahead of time. Decide on a food that everybody in the family likes, be it ever so humble! Give everyone a part in the preparation. At mealtime, ask your child to take the bread received at the *Communal Ritual Celebration*, solemnly break it and pass a piece to each family member. No words are necessary; just enjoy your meal together.

We help prepare meals.

●● **Parent Notes**

Look at the pictures above and identify what is happening in each. Then talk with your child about the many ways people share in preparing meals. You might ask, **How does Mother help?** *What does Dad do? How do you help to prepare for the meals? How do you feel when you know you've helped?*

We enjoy meals together.

I like to share meals with _____

_____

_____.

●● Look at the pictures of family and friends sharing meals together, and ask your child what these people in each picture are sharing. (Food, drink, conversation, jokes, plans, dreams.)

In the space provided above have your child write the names of people he or she likes to share meals with. Then ask your child to imagine that he or she invited these people to a meal. Ask,

What would you share at the meal to show how much you liked these people?

Some meals are special.

●● *Have your child identify the occasions the people in the picture are celebrating. Ask,* **What signs or actions show what is being celebrated? How do we know who is being remembered?**

Talk with your child about some of the events your family celebrates with special meals. How does everybody share to help make the meal special? How are your family's festive meals the same as those pictured? How are they different?

33

The Last Supper

On the night before he died,
Jesus ate supper with his Apostles.
During the meal, Jesus took bread,
blessed it, broke it,
and gave it to his friends.

●● *Point out that Jesus shared many meals with others. Perhaps your child knows of some stories about Jesus and his friends sharing meals.*

Use the picture above to introduce the story of the Last Supper. Ask your child to tell the story in his or her own words, then read the story with your child.

"Take this and eat," Jesus said.
"This is my Body. Do this in memory of me."
After eating, Jesus took a cup of wine.
He blessed the wine, and gave it to his friends.
Jesus said, "This is my Blood, which will be
given for you."

adapted from Luke 22:14-20

●● Talk about the story with your child, and help him or her to see that Jesus loved his friends very much and that he wanted to share more with them than food and drink. He wanted to give them a way to always remember him and his love. Ask, **What words show that Jesus gave himself? What did Jesus do with the bread? What did he do with the wine? What do you think Jesus meant when he said,** "Do this in memory of me?"

Gather the idea of this session together by helping your child identify that Jesus gave himself to his apostles in this special way at a meal—the Last Supper. At Jesus' command we continue to share the Body and Blood of Jesus in our Sunday celebration of the Eucharist.

Jesus shares his life in a meal.

Jesus wants us to know how much he loves us. Jesus shares himself with us in a special meal. Soon I,

_____,

will be ready to share the meal of Jesus.

Blessed are you, Lord our God, for Jesus your son. You ask us to remember that Jesus is always our friend. Jesus gives himself to us in a special meal of Bread and Wine. Thank-you, God, for all the love you share.

Amen.

●● *Have your child read and print his or her name in the blank above to complete the sentence. Then conclude this session with the blessing prayer.*

Looking Ahead to Sunday

Tell your child he or she will be given a small loaf of bread at Mass next Sunday. Your child will then be asked to share the bread at the meal at home with the family. This bread will be a reminder of the life shared and given among your family.

4.
We Celebrate as God's Thankful Family

Blessed are you, O Lord.
You make us Easter people.
You give us special times to celebrate.
You send Jesus to help us remember your love.
You invite us to share the special meal of Jesus.
We thank you, Lord, for all your gifts,
and we bless your name forever.
Amen.

Aim

The children will recognize that we remember Jesus in the celebration of the Eucharist. We share in Jesus' life-giving presence in a festive meal of Bread and Wine.

Overview

In the third family session you and your child looked at the way Jesus asks us to remember him. By reading the story of the Last Supper, you saw how Jesus wants to share himself with us, and how he gives us his presence in Bread and Wine in the setting of a festive meal. Jesus said, "Do this to remember me." His command was first carried out by the apostles after the Easter experience. Since we are their heirs, Jesus' gift to them is our birthright as well. When we gather as they did, we also share in Jesus' life-giving supper. We call this gathering the eucharistic liturgy or the Mass.

Over the centuries the form of the Mass has varied greatly, but its central meaning and reality remain constant. On Sunday, the special—the "different"—day of the week, we gather to celebrate God's love for us by remembering Jesus. We share a meal in which we believe Jesus is present today: in our gathering, in one another, in God's Word, in the broken bread and shared cup of blessing. We believe that by sharing in this celebration we're nourished in body and in spirit and thus are helped and called to give thanks by sharing God's love with all we meet.

Your child has already experienced Sunday as a special day, a day your family celebrates together. Your child has learned that Sunday is special because it's the day of Jesus' resurrection. In session two your family remembered people through stories, actions, and things. Together you discovered that through remembering, people can be present to us, even if they're physically absent. You and your child also recalled events in the life of Jesus and learned how Jesus asks us to remember God's love. Finally, in the third session, your child learned that Jesus gives us himself in a meal and asks us to celebrate this meal in memory of him. Through your child's own experience of festive and family meals, and through listening to the story of the Last Supper, your child realized that we remember Jesus and share his life-giving presence in a festive meal of Bread and Wine.

In this concluding session you'll investigate the eucharistic liturgy, the Mass. You'll discover that each week there is a gathering of God's family on our special day—Sunday. You'll see that the Mass remembers Jesus in word and action and celebrates his presence in a festive meal in which we're invited to share. Finally, you'll also see how the Mass calls us to continue thanking God by commissioning us to share his love with others.

At the very beginning of the Mass, Christians are invited to gather as a people who share membership in God's family. The priest's words of greeting and welcome signal this divine invitation: "In the name of the Father, and of the Son, and of the Holy Spirit." Our signing of ourselves with the cross and our "Amen" proclaim our acceptance of the Lord's invitation and our acknowledgment that we are indeed his children. The readings of the Mass (the Liturgy of the Word), especially the Gospel, help us remember Jesus. We witness that this really is "Good News" by standing to hear it, with song or with incense, and by our acclamation of praise: "Praise to you, Lord Jesus Christ." We also remember Jesus in the meal he gives us. In the Eucharistic Prayer the priest prays the words Jesus spoke at the Last Supper. We fulfill Jesus' command to "Do this to remember me." At the conclusion of the Eucharistic Prayer the priest lifts the Bread and Wine and invites us to proclaim our belief in Jesus' presence and to offer God praise (the Doxology). This we do by saying or singing: "Amen" (the Great Amen). At Communion time we share in the meal Jesus gives us. We eat the Bread and drink the Wine which is Jesus present among us. The priest or other minister of Communion presents the Bread and Wine to us with the words, "The Body of Christ," "The Blood of Christ." With faith and joy we respond: "Amen!" ("Yes, I believe!")

As Mass draws to a close, we're sent forth to share with others the love and life we've celebrated. "Eucharist" means "thanksgiving." The best way we say "thank you" for a special gift is to share its benefits with others. We know from our own experience that gifts are given to be enjoyed and shared. In the Concluding Rites of the Mass we're reminded that Jesus wants us to share his presence with others. We're dismissed with God's blessing and with a commission to give thanks for this celebration by sharing its joy with others: "Go in peace to love and serve the Lord." We announce our willingness to fulfill this mandate with our grateful response, "Thanks be to God."

By reviewing the Mass with your child in this way, he or she will realize how the Mass celebrates Jesus' presence among us. Your child will see how we gather as God's family on a special day each week to remember Jesus in word and action, and to share his presence in a festive meal. Finally, your child will discover that the Mass calls us to continue to thank God for his love given in Jesus, through our resolve to share that love with others.

We gather on Sunday.

We gather at _____

_____ Church.

Father _____
welcomes us in God's name.

**In the name of the Father,
and of the Son
and of the Holy Spirit.**

We say: _____.

●● **Parent Notes**

Briefly recall that your family marks Sunday in special ways, and the most important way you celebrate is to worship at Sunday Mass. Have your child complete the sentences on this page which tell the name of the church where you celebrate the Eucharist, and the name of your pastor.

Explain that when we gather at Mass, the Presider (priest) greets us in God's name and welcomes us as members of God's family (session one.) Have your child read the words of the priest's welcome. Then ask, **When Father says these words, what do we do?** (We make the sign of the cross.) **What do** we say? (Amen.) **What does "Amen" mean?** (Yes, I believe.) Have your child write "Amen" on the third blank line on this page.

We remember Jesus in the Word.

We thank God for letting
us remember
Jesus in his Word.

We say:

_____

_____

_____ .

●● Recall that your family remembers stories about people who are special to them (session two). To help your child recognize that as members of God's family we remember stories about Jesus during Mass, ask, **What is the priest in the picture doing?** (He's reading or proclaiming the Gospel.) **Do you know what the word "gospel" means?** (It means good news.) **How do we show**

that we believe the Gospel is good news? (We stand at attention, introduce the Gospel with words of praise, listen intently, use incense sometimes.)

Help your child fill in the blank above with the response after the proclamation of the Gospel: Praise to you, Lord Jesus Christ.

We remember Jesus in a special meal.

Take this, all of you,
and eat it:
this is my Body which
will be given up for you.

Take this, all of you,
and drink from it:
this is the cup of my Blood,
the Blood of the new
and everlasting covenant.

Do this in memory of me.

●● *From your family experiences your child knows that you celebrate special occasions together and remember people and events (session three).*

*Recall that Jesus celebrated a special meal with his friends. Ask, **What did Jesus do at the Last Supper?** Then, direct your child to the picture and words above.*

To help your child focus on the Eucharist as the continuation of Jesus' command to "do this in memory of me," read the words with your child. Point out that at Mass the priest takes the Bread and Wine and says the same words Jesus said at the Last Supper. Tell your child that Jesus comes to us in the Bread and Wine.

We sing our faith.

Through him, with him, in him,
in the unity of the Holy Spirit,
all glory and honor is yours,
almighty Father,
for ever and ever.

We thank God for Jesus
who comes to us
in Bread and Wine.

We sing _____.

•• *We thank God for this gift of Jesus by responding to the priest's words (Through him . . . .) Ask your child to write the word we sing which means "Yes, we truly believe that this is Jesus." (Amen.)*

We share the meal of Jesus.

The Body of Christ.

We say _____.
　　　　　Yes, I believe.

The Blood of Christ.

We say _____.
　　　　　Yes, I believe.

●● *To help your child see that we all share in the meal of Jesus at Communion time by eating the Bread (and drinking the Wine), ask your child to tell what is happening in the pictures on this page.*

Have your child read what the Minister of Communion says to us when we come to Communion. Ask, **What do we say before we receive either the Bread or the Wine?** *(Amen.) Have your child write the response in the space provided.*

We give God thanks in our lives.

Go in peace to love and serve the Lord.

We say _____

_____.

●● *Explain to your child that as Mass ends, the priest invites us to go forth to share with others the joy we've celebrated. Have your child read the words of the priest. Then ask,* **What does the priest ask us to do?** *(Go in peace to love and serve the Lord.)* **What do we say?** *(Thanks be to God.)*

Have your child write the response in the spaces provided.

Each week on a special day
We remember Jesus in a special way.
Our family joins with others
To listen to God's story.

We remember how Jesus died for us
And was raised to life in glory.

We share the meal he gives us,
Himself in Bread and Wine.

We thank God for his special gift.
The gift that's yours and mine.

This is how I will share God's gift with others:

_____

_____.

Blessed are you, Lord our God.
We thank you for the gift of Jesus.
We ask you to make us ready
to remember Jesus and share his
special meal with all the members
of your family.
Amen.

●● *Read together the above poem. Share your own faith that we thank God best by serving others in our everyday lives. Have your child decide on one specific, loving action he or she can do which will carry the command to "go in peace to love and serve the Lord."*

Looking Ahead to Sunday

This coming Sunday your child will be given a formal invitation to join the parish community in First Communion.

Paste your invitation here.

Paste your certificate here.

My First Communion
Picture.